31143009924359
J SP 567.915 Mattern, J
Mattern, Joanne.
Triceratops =

DISCARDED

RICHMOND PUBLIC LIBRARY

Trav

P9-ECW-999

Let's Read About Dinosaurs/
Conozcamos a los dinosaurios

Triceratops/
Triceratops

by Joanne Mattern

Illustrations by Jeffrey Mangiat

Reading consultant: Susan Nations, M.Ed., author,
literacy coach, consultant in literacy development

Science consultant: Philip J. Currie, Ph.D., Professor and Canada Research Chair
of Dinosaur Palaeobiology at the University of Alberta, Canada

WEEKLY READER®
PUBLISHING

Please visit our web site at: www.garethstevens.com
For a free color catalog describing ourlist of high-quality books,
call 1-800-542-2595 (USA) or 1-800-387-3178 (Canada).
Our fax: 1-877-542-2596.

Library of Congress Cataloging-in-Publication Data available upon request from publisher.
Fax (414) 336-0157 for the attention of the Publishing Records Department.

ISBN-13: 978-0-8368-8021-2 (lib. bdg.)
ISBN-13: 978-0-8368-8028-1 (softcover)

This edition first published in 2007 by
Weekly Reader® Books
An Imprint of Gareth Stevens Publishing
1 Reader's Digest Road
Pleasantville, NY 10570-7000 USA

Copyright © 2007 by Weekly Reader® Early Learning Library

Managing editor: Valerie J. Weber
Art direction, cover and layout design: Tammy West
Spanish translation: Tatiana Acosta and Guillermo Gutiérrez

All rights reserved. No part of this book may be reproduced, stored in a retrieval system, or
transmitted in any form or by any means, electronic, mechanical, photocopying, recording,
or otherwise, without the prior written permission of the copyright holder.

Printed in the United States of America

2 3 4 5 6 7 8 9 10 10 09

Note to Educators and Parents

Reading is such an exciting adventure for young children! They are beginning to integrate their oral language skills with written language. To encourage children along the path to early literacy, books must be colorful, engaging, and interesting; they should invite the young reader to explore both the print and the pictures.

Let's Read about Dinosaurs is a new series designed to help children read about some of their favorite — and most fearsome — animals. In each book, young readers will learn how each dinosaur survived so long ago.

Each book is specially designed to support the young reader in the reading process. The familiar topics are appealing to young children and invite them to read — and re-read — again and again. The full-color photographs and enhanced text further support the student during the reading process.

In addition to serving as wonderful picture books in schools, libraries, homes, and other places where children learn to love reading, these books are specifically intended to be read within an instructional guided reading group. This small group setting allows beginning readers to work with a fluent adult model as they make meaning from the text. After children develop fluency with the text and content, the book can be read independently. Children and adults alike will find these books supportive, engaging, and fun!

— Susan Nations, M.Ed., author, literacy coach,
and consultant in literacy development

Nota para los maestros y los padres

¡Leer es una aventura tan emocionante para los niños pequeños! A esta edad están comenzando a integrar su manejo del lenguaje oral con el lenguaje escrito. Para animar a los niños en el camino de la lectura incipiente, los libros deben ser coloridos, estimulantes e interesantes; deben invitar a los jóvenes lectores a explorar la letra impresa y las ilustraciones.

Conozcamos a los dinosaurios es una nueva colección diseñada para presentar a los niños información sobre algunos de sus animales favoritos — y más temibles. En cada libro, los jóvenes lectores aprenderán cómo sobrevivió hace tanto tiempo un dinosaurio.

Cada libro está especialmente diseñado para ayudar a los jóvenes lectores en el proceso de lectura. Los temas familiares llaman la atención de los niños y los invitan a leer una y otra vez. Las fotografías a todo color y el tamaño de la letra ayudan aún más al estudiante en el proceso de lectura.

Además de servir como maravillosos libros ilustrados en escuelas, bibliotecas, hogares y otros lugares donde los niños aprenden a amar la lectura, estos libros han sido especialmente concebidos para ser leídos en un grupo de lectura guiada. Este contexto permite que los lectores incipientes trabajen con un adulto que domina la lectura mientras van determinando el significado del texto. Una vez que los niños dominan el texto y el contenido, el libro puede ser leído de manera independiente. ¡Estos libros les resultarán útiles, estimulantes y divertidos a niños y a adultos por igual!

— Susan Nations, M.Ed., autora, tutora de alfabetización
y consultora de desarrollo de la lectura

Look at the three horns on
this dinosaur's face! This is
Triceratops (try-SER-uh-tops).
Its name means "three-horned
face."

¡Mira los tres cuernos en
la cara de este dinosaurio!
Es un triceratops. Su nombre
significa "cara con tres cuernos".

horns/
cuernos

5

Triceratops was a big dinosaur.
It weighed as much as three cars.
It was as long as two cars.

El triceratops era un dinosaurio
grande. Pesaba lo mismo que
tres autos. Era tan largo como
dos autos.

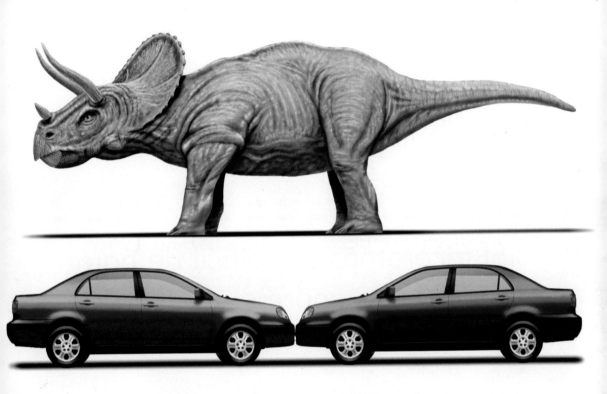

Triceratops was hard to stop!
Although it was huge, it could
still run fast.

━ ━ ━ ━ ━ ━ ━ ━ ━ ━ ━ ━ ━

¡El triceratops era difícil de parar!
Aunque era enorme, era capaz
de correr muy deprisa.

Its horns also kept Triceratops safe. These sharp spikes helped Triceratops defend itself.

- - - - - - - - - - - - - - - -

El triceratops también usaba los cuernos como protección. Esas puntas afiladas le servían para defenderse.

A bony **frill** grew on the back of its head. The frill kept other dinosaurs from biting its neck.

- - - - - - - - - - - - - -

En la parte de atrás de la cabeza tenía una **gorguera** ósea. Esa gorguera impedía que otros dinosaurios le mordieran en el cuello.

frill/gorguera

13

Its thick skin also protected
Triceratops from other dinosaurs.
It was not hard enough to stop
a T. rex from biting it though!

Su dura piel también protegía al
triceratops de otros dinosaurios.
¡Sin embargo, no era lo bastante
dura para no ser atravesada por
los dientes de un T. rex!

Triceratops ate plants. It ripped off leaves and twigs with its mouth. Then it chewed them with its strong back teeth.

-- -- -- -- -- -- -- -- -- -- -- --

El triceratops comía plantas. Arrancaba con la boca hojas y ramitas. Después, las masticaba con sus fuertes dientes posteriores.

Scientists think Triceratops traveled in groups. These groups were called **herds**. The herd moved from place to place looking for plants to eat.

Los científicos piensan que los triceratops se desplazaban en grupos. Estos grupos reciben el nombre de **manadas**.
La manada iba de un lugar a otro en busca de plantas para comer.

19

Triceratops died out long ago. Today we can see models of this dinosaur in museums.

– – – – – – – – – – – – – – –

Los triceratops desaparecieron hace mucho tiempo. Hoy podemos ver modelos de este dinosaurio en los museos.

TRICERATOPS

21

Glossary

defend — to protect from danger or hurt
frill — a strip of bone with a curved edge
herds — large groups of animals
models — copies of an animal, person, or object
museums — places where interesting objects are shown to the public
scientists — people who study nature

Glosario

científicos — personas que estudian la naturaleza
defenderse — protegerse de un peligro o daño
gorguera — tira ósea con un borde curvo
manadas — grupos grandes de animales
modelos — copias de un animal, una persona o un objeto
museos — lugares donde se muestran al público objetos interesantes

For More Information/ Más información

Books/Libros

I Wonder Why Triceratops Had Horns and Other Questions about Dinosaurs. Ron Theodorou (Kingfisher)

¿Qué clase de dinosaurio soy? Aventuras jurásicas (serie). John Patience (Silver Dolphin en español)

Triceratops. Helen Frost (Pebble Plus)

Triceratops: Mighty Three-Horned Dinosaur. I Like Dinosaurs! (series). Michael Skrepnick (Enslow)

Watch Out, Triceratops. Dawn Bentley (Soundprints)

Index/Índice

About the Author

Joanne Mattern has written more than 150 books for children. She has written about weird animals, sports, world cities, dinosaurs, and many other subjects. Joanne also works in her local library. She lives in New York State with her husband, three daughters, and assorted pets. She enjoys animals, music, going to baseball games, reading, and visiting schools to talk about her books.

Información sobre la autora

Joanne Mattern ha escrito más de ciento cincuenta libros para niños. Ha escrito textos sobre animales extraños, deportes, ciudades del mundo, dinosaurios y muchos otros temas. Además, Joanne trabaja en la biblioteca de su comunidad. Vive en el estado de Nueva York con su esposo, sus tres hijas y varias mascotas. A Joanne le gustan los animales, la música, ir al béisbol, leer y hacer visitas a las escuelas para hablar de sus libros.